Why Not STRETCH?

A Roadmap to Overcome Barriers Leading to College

Theresa Smith

DEDICATION

Son, when I first laid eyes on you, my vision of you made my purpose clearer. Now, my willingness to stretch exceeds my initial goals. You are, and forever will be, the motivation behind every stretch.

9-15-2018 to beyond

Why Not Stretch? A Roadmap to Overcome Barriers Leading to College
Copyright © 2021 by Theresa Smith
ISBN 9781645382256
First Edition

Why Not Stretch? A Roadmap to Overcome Barriers Leading to College
by Theresa Smith

For information, please contact:

www.ten16press.com
Waukesha, WI

CONTENTS

Preface

Dear Reader,

Finances were already a stretch for me, and it was going to cost four hundred dollars a month to bring my private student loans current, but I couldn't afford that. I was years out of college and, at the time, I wasn't making much money, only enough to sustain the high rent in Chicago. The thought of defaulting on my student loans sent me into a spiral of depression. *How would this affect my credit? My future home and car? Vacations?* Life was in jeopardy, and I had to learn how to stretch my mind in a totally different way.

So, there I was, left to reflect on how I ended up in this financial disaster. If I had only began stretching my mindset prior to entering college, then I would have been in a better place after I walked across the stage and earned my degree. You see, I learned a lot about the college-going process while in college and while paying for college. It would have been much cheaper if I had stretched to become a more self-directed, and self-empowered individual prior to college. But I didn't, and this lack of self-knowledge would create some discomfort when it came to creating a repayment plan.

Today as a financial aid counselor, I see all types of students who have gotten themselves into the same situation I was in. Even many

K-12 educators share with me how they wish students were taught certain tools to be successful in college prior to going, because once you get to college, it is expected that you are knowledgeable enough to navigate all of its intricate processes. In the midst of those discussions, I'm often left wondering about all of the students who would have graduated before such education reform had taken place.

With much prayer and motivation, I began to think and write about those students and my own journey through the college-going process. As a high school student, I required more than a workbook that told me when and how to apply for admission and financial aid. I needed a step-by-step proven system that would connect what I needed to do in high school with my future goals and role as a college student. I needed a workbook that could make the results of poor decision-making **REAL** to me so I would be encouraged to stretch my thinking, planning, and behavior.

This workbook does just that. With the end goal in mind, students will learn to be intentional and self-directed with how they navigate high school and be more prepared for college. The more prepared you are, the less likely you are to make the financial mistakes that I've made and that I see students make every day. In addition to being prepared for college, the lessons you will learn in this workbook can be applied to every area of your life.

Due to the number of jewels dropped in this workbook, I HIGHLY recommend you take your time to dissect each chapter. I don't want you to feel overwhelmed, so please take your time! Read, discuss, and reflect on what is being offered with a friend, mentor, or family member. If you are one of the above, make sure you sit down with your college-bound student to make sure the content is being absorbed and understood by them.

Lastly, I ask the question: *Why not stretch?* You have nothing to lose and so much to gain! By stretching the way you think of and see the college process, you have the power to become a better version of yourself while navigating the difficult process of higher education. My hope is that my own story inspires you to stretch beyond norms, curriculum and the opinions of others so that you find freedom in financial stability while attaining a college degree.

Ready. Set. Stretch.
Everything you are about to read is going to help you to become a great college student. No matter if it is about finding motivation or choosing who to hang around, successful students typically stretch in every area of their lives. So, are you ready to STRETCH?

Stretched-
Stretch-
Stretching

To stretch is to be capable of being made longer or wider without tearing. It is to expand one's vision, thinking, or movement beyond what you may see, think, or feel. Stretching typically occurs when  you are uncomfortable, so that you ultimately become comfortable.

The Journey to Stretching

I am angry! No, not someone cut me off while driving angry. But a trapped-in-a-cage- while-hungry-surrounded-by-food-that-I-can't-touch angry. I'm stressing out. Bags are around my eyes, I'm isolating myself, and I feel hopeless. Although it may look like I have it together, I'm crumbling on the inside. I'm desperately awaiting sunlight, a new day, and a change to come my way. Yes, I have my bachelor's degree and yes, I have a master's degree. And yes, I have a job that requires at least one of those degrees. But what do those degrees mean when the happiness of accomplishing something so great is quickly swept away by the giant storm following me wherever I go?

I began writing today out of anger. I'm not sure if I should be mad at the "system," public schools, my parents, or grandparents. All I know is that I worked hard to get my education so I could help students. I could not be effective without my degrees, so going to college wasn't a bad idea. My plan was to graduate, get a good job, and work my way up. Everything is going as planned; however, I still have this cloud over me. My master's degree is in hand, and my student loans are now in repayment. My loans! My stupid loans that I used to pay for school are hovering over and suffocating me. I can't seem to enjoy anything for an extended period of time without being faced with reality; my loans are sucking the life out of me.

? Have you ever done everything you were supposed to do, only to be faced with more barriers, problems, and stress? Feel free to write your thoughts below:

? How did you react? Did you keep moving forward because you understood that everyone has problems, but only the strong or successful confront their problems and don't allow them to hinder their goal? Express your thoughts below:

? Did you do something negative because life isn't fair?

? Explain how you react to problems. Does your reaction help you reach your goals, or does it hold you back?

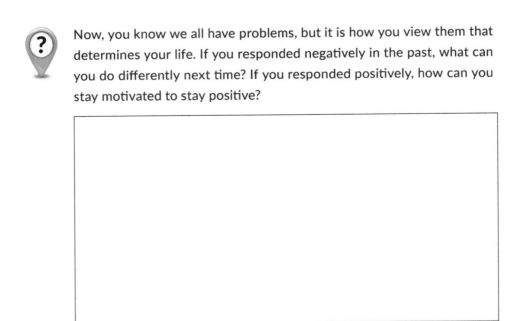

Now, you know we all have problems, but it is how you view them that determines your life. If you responded negatively in the past, what can you do differently next time? If you responded positively, how can you stay motivated to stay positive?

I wish being angry would solve all of my problems, but it will not. It would be easy for me to blame my grandparents for not showing my parents, who had the responsibility of showing me, how to make smart decisions regarding my college-going process. Yes, it is very easy to point the blame at anyone but ourselves when it comes to why we are not in the position we believe we should be in.

As I write this, politicians are discussing the funding of schools. In Illinois, what each public school is given financially is not always based upon what the student needs, but rather what the state can afford. Your resources and opportunities for a better education may be in the hands of someone who cannot identify with your struggle. It may be in the hands of a state that has to take budget cuts. School books may be outdated and classrooms may be oversized. With all that is going on, you must ask yourself, *Do I wait for our leaders to get it together for MY life* (keep in mind that they may not get it together until after you graduate), *or do I take control of MY future, since I am the one that has to live with it anyway?*

You may have been neglected or abused in your childhood, raised in a single parent household, introduced to drugs, given up on school, or maybe all of the above. Many of us have had to experience situations that I wouldn't wish on anyone. It is very unfortunate, but just as I'm using my anger to help someone, we must be able to do the same for ourselves. We must be able to turn our bad into good. We must start now and continue to do so over and over and over again, as life is filled with many ups and downs. So, please don't allow the bad things that happen in your life to prevent you from having a good life.

The loan companies won't listen to, "No one helped me through the college process, so I spent too much time trying to figure it out while my loans were

EXAMPLE

stacking up" stories. They will not erase loans because of an unfortunate situation. They do not care that I was misinformed about the financial aid process. All they care about is whether or not my bill is paid on time.

The same goes for you! If you sit around and complain about your childhood, what are you accomplishing? Nothing will change for you. Complaining will not get you anywhere. It is up to you to make a change. We all must change. While the politicians were arguing about education reform, I decided to put my anger and passion to work.

 # "I will make it. The 'IT' part is up to me!"

So, if you will repeat after me: I, (insert name here)_____ , will not throw a pity party about my past, current situation, upbringing, circumstances, or surroundings. I cannot wait around for politicians to make decisions about my education. I am the captain of my fate. I will make it. The "IT" part is up to me!

Where do you begin? When I was in high school, I didn't have counselors reaching out to me to help me with life after high school. I mean, I was barely passing (*It's never too late to turn your life around*). Hmmm, I could definitely blame them for my mistakes, but how would that help me? It was my senior year, and all of my peers were receiving acceptance letters into colleges, and I hadn't applied to one. Needless to say, my peers motivated me to begin exploring my options.

Motivation

I believe that motivation is a good place to start! What motivates you to change your future? Remember, both negative and positive things, people, and circumstances can be great motivators. It may be easy to think of possible motivators, but we want to write them down, like right here on this page!

    Once you find your motivation (your "why,"), hold on to it. Write it down in various places. It will serve as a constant reminder of why you are stretching.

    Having motivation will get you started, but in order to truly stretch, you must believe that you can. The next step is to get your mind right.

Brain, Cerebral, MIND

Have you ever heard the slogan, "A mind is a terrible thing to waste"? That slogan comes from the United Negro College Fund, and it points out how powerful your mind is. It is so powerful that if you don't use it, you lose the ability to control your life.

Let's test the power of the mind. Think of your favorite food.

Are you thinking of it? Picturing it in your mind?

The act of *thinking* about your favorite food will have you tasting it, smelling it, and maybe making plans to get it after reading this. You see how powerful your mind is? The great part about your mind is that you control it.

I had some of the worst grades in high school. Going from a normal middle school to a college-bound high school where they really prepared you for college by assigning college work, I found myself to be underprepared. Everyone seemed to be getting algebra, but I struggled. My mom told me that I could do it, but that wasn't enough. I had to psych myself out by telling myself that I was smart, although I didn't *feel* smart. To my surprise, it worked! My new confidence led me to stay after class every day with my teacher until I got it. There was no more psyching myself out. I was smart.

Once I gained confidence, I was then able to comfortably ask questions in class without thinking that other people thought I was dumb. Bottomline, they don't determine who I am or how smart I am. Their opinions of me don't matter, because they are not in charge of my future!

Maybe everyone has on designer clothes and you don't; or has the latest technology, but you don't; or maybe you don't feel as smart as the other students. Sometimes when we feel alone in a situation because of those things, we begin to isolate ourselves. We may begin to lose confidence in speaking up. If you allow those things to get in the way of your learning, you will not be able to gain the necessary confidence in yourself to produce a better you!

STRETCH

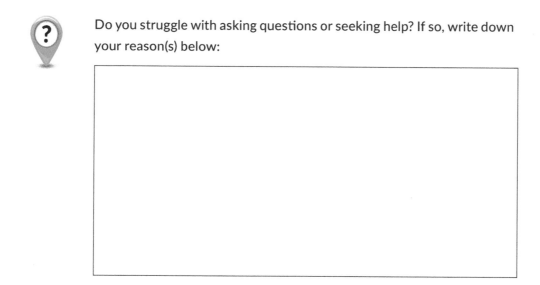

Do you struggle with asking questions or seeking help? If so, write down your reason(s) below:

In life, and especially while trying to navigate the college-going process, you have to get comfortable with asking questions. Those that ask questions get the help needed to succeed. I believe that you DESERVE the answers. If you believe you do, too, then make sure you ASK as many questions as you would like. If you struggle with asking questions, try writing them down as they come to mind, then practice asking them in a mirror until you become comfortable.

EXAMPLE I began asking questions about chapter three. The more questions I asked, I found that my problem came from not fully understanding chapter one. I knew then that I had to get tutoring on chapter one in order to complete chapter three. When you ask a lot of questions, you discover where the root of the problem lies. So, ask away!

After you have put your mind to it, you must prepare to demonstrate discipline, determination, and endurance. If I had only psyched myself out by believing that I could do the math, I would not have received a B in the class. I had to discipline myself to stay after class while all my girls were hanging out. I had to push myself to keep trying, even when I wasn't getting it. I can teach anyone about discipline or endurance, but determination, that is something I can't teach. Determination has to come from within. You have to choose to win, to keep fighting, and to want a better life badly enough. You determine how determined you are. Your actions, especially when faced with obstacles, show how determined you are. I was so determined to turn my grade around in that class that I not only believed it, but my actions also showed it. I developed the ability to block out all unimportant things that would disrupt me from learning algebra. I learned to visualize myself at the finish line. This is what kept me going. This was a skill I developed and still use this very day.

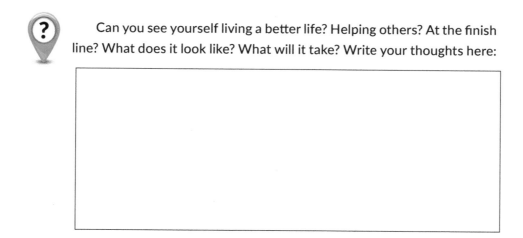 Can you see yourself living a better life? Helping others? At the finish line? What does it look like? What will it take? Write your thoughts here:

Now that your mind is made up, what's next? How do you keep moving forward when you've fallen behind on assignments, have trouble at home, or no one seems to have your back? Remember, you are in charge of your destiny. Do the best you can and make sure to build your own community of support. You may have already started doing this, but if you haven't, this would be your next step.

Building Your Community

I have to admit, the best decision I made was to ask select people along my journey to be my mentors.

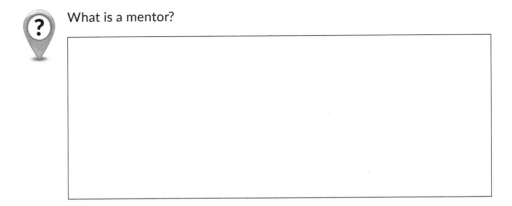

What is a mentor?

I did not choose people who were always involved in drama or lacked a high school diploma—even if they were my family or friends. Family and friends do typically have good advice, but most people will offer advice because they don't want to see you make the same mistakes they did. If you are asking for advice, try to choose people who fought through their own problems to reach their dreams. If the people in your inner circle haven't overcome their own obstacles, I don't suggest making them your first choice for mentors (although you can still respect their opinions). My mentors are the ones who I could lean on for encouragement. They understood the processes and problems one may face while trying to reach a goal. Most importantly, they knew what to do to push past those problems, what resources could help, and which fellow friends in the field could assist me in moving forward.

Mentor
Who should be your mentor? How do you ask them? What happens next?

Your mentor can be anyone in your school, neighborhood, church, etc. If you connect with a positive figure in any one of those areas, ask them! Ask them to become your mentor. I have asked people to be my mentor in each place that I just named. It's quite normal to have more than one, just make sure your mentor has something that you want and aspire to be.

How do you ask someone to be your mentor? Let me assist you with that since I have done this countless times. I have stopped them on a lunch break or during

STRETCH

a normal conversation between myself and them to simply say, "I admire the person you are. I don't have much guidance in this area, and I was wondering if you would be my mentor?" All of the people I have asked did not hesitate to say yes. I didn't think they would say no since I could tell that they found interest in me.

When you look for someone to become your mentor, what should attract you to that individual is just the natural connection you two have. There is no science to it. Some of us click better together than others. If you have a connection, the natural assumption is that that person cares for you. Your mentor should care about you. If they always inquire about your well-being or get on your case when you are not performing to your best ability, then they are showing you that they care. Your mentor should encourage you to be better, and ultimately, they should believe in you. The perfect mentor is someone who is honest with you. They don't tell you things just to make you feel good, but because they want what is best for you. Their advice may not make you feel good at the moment, but it will help you in the long run.

Your mentor should be someone who is successful in your eyes. They are your mentor for a reason: you want to one day be like them. This doesn't mean that you want to be a teacher, although one of your mentors may be a teacher. This may mean that you want a degree and your teacher has a degree, so he or she can help you with that process. Again, you can choose multiple mentors. I have one that is where I want to be professionally, spiritually, and one who is just someone who pushes me and encourages me to be the best me that I can be. Their words should match their actions. I can't tell you how to fish if I have never fished. They should be able to teach and show you how to be successful. They should be able to tell you *why* you should or shouldn't do something.

 Do you have someone in mind? List them here.

1)
2)
3)
4)
5)
6)

I was terrible at math in high school, but I wanted to be a dentist. My mentor at the time would tell me to explore other options as well, since going to dental school meant I would have to complete a lot of math courses.

STRETCH

She forced me to think realistically but did not shoot down my dreams, just in case.

GOOD MENTOR

I continued to pursue dentistry, although math was a struggle. My mentor encouraged me to stay after class for extra help, and I was able to finally understand math.

MENTEE

My mentor helped me to come up with a plan. She taught me what was required of someone who was in that field. Once I determined that I still wanted to pursue dentistry, she helped me to understand the importance of hard work.

LESSON

Once you have your mentor, it is important that they are committed to you and you're just as committed to learning from them. Your blood family are not the only ones capable of showing such loyalty. Give your mentor a chance to help you and become open to new ideas. I know it may be hard being open with someone who is not family, but if you take the time to build a relationship, make sure you begin to tell them more and more about yourself. This helps your mentor to guide you better. It also makes them aware that you are trusting them. They should be equally as open and transparent. Some of the best advice I have ever received from my mentors has been through their personal journeys. This type of openness comes with time and commitment to learning.

As you are getting to know each other, it is important that your mentor believes in you. They must see that you have potential. When someone believes in you, they invest in you. They invest time, effort, and sometimes money. I know that my mentors believe in me because they encourage me to become involved in projects that I would have never done by myself. They push me to think past my own experiences, and when they introduce me, they do it with a smile on their face. If someone tells you that you can't do something without assisting you to find other options or routes to get to what you would like to do (and your gut says that you can), you may need to find another mentor. If you are being told that you can become better and that you may have your heart's desire, keep that mentor. Just make sure they are not all talk, but that they can help you come up with a goal or define your dream by turning it into reality.

Your mentor should do more than just believe in you, they should help you reach your goals. If you are unsure of what you want to be, they should help you come up with options based upon your strengths, likes, dislikes, passions, and dreams. Not only should they help you come up with options, but also a plan. Your mentor may help you identify things in you that you may not have been aware of. If your strengths lead you to being a doctor, although you frown at the thought of being a doctor, you have a right to decline that suggestion. Just because your mentor may say you should or should not achieve a goal does not mean you have to go with it. Your voice is important in this process, too. Your mentor is there to encourage and assist you with YOUR journey. They don't determine it. You ultimately have the final say over your life.

As a mentee, you must be able to take criticism. A good mentor will help you to make realistic goals, but if your heart is set on something, do not allow anyone to talk you out of it. Your mentor should be able to help you identify the appropriate steps you will need to take to increase your chances of achieving your goal. I had to first attend tutoring after school every day with Mr. McCullum until I understood algebra. My mentor's encouragement to seek help helped me to get on the right path toward dentistry.

Once you have mentors, it is important to note that they have lives, too. It is easy to feel like they are not there after establishing the working relationship between you two. Some may be more hands-on than others, but from my experience, and now from being a mentor myself, we like to be reached out to as well. I may ask my mentees out for lunch every once in a while, but the majority of the time, they reach out to me. I do the same with my mentor. She is a very busy woman, so when I need assistance or just want to catch up, I don't hesitate to call or email her. We always make time, and I always leave our meetings with notes (I always come prepared with paper and pen) and a new outlook. You are not a burden to someone who agrees to assist you. It is your responsibility to use your resource and keep the lines of communication open.

Now that you, like myself, have your mentor(s) in place (you can select more along your journey), we must examine the friends you have. They are a part of your personal community as well. Who can forget your friends? Good friends are hard to come by, so how many of us have them?

Friends

It is very important that you surround yourself with positive people and friends. If they are not positive or working hard to have a better life for themselves, my friend, you must show them to the nearest exit. This realization is key. You are who you surround yourself with. If you find your "friends" being negative more than positive (not the constructive criticism we talked about earlier) or pressuring you to do things that could potentially land you failing, in jail, with kids, poor, or dead, you may want to distance yourself from them. This doesn't mean you can't have fun. Good fun is when you don't end up in trouble from doing it.

I have friends who decided to become exotic dancers. This change for them did not occur overnight. At one point, they wanted to be nurses, teachers, etc. They wanted more out of life (and still do), but they chose the quickest route to fast cash.

PUBLIC SERVICE ANNOUNCEMENT
Fast cash doesn't last long!

We had many great memories together that I can't and will not forget. Since they chose this lifestyle, we haven't remained as close. I check in on them every now and then, and we have remained friendly, but that's it. Their desire for fast cash could possibly rub off on me. I could easily lose sight of my goals because I see them in nice cars and clothes. Is it that serious? Yes! Whenever you try to change your life for the better, there will always be roadblocks, people that seem like they are doing better than you, and temptation to get you off the path to a better you. Whether they try to persuade you or not, it's hard to deny things like fast cash when you are a broke college student.

NEWSFLASH
The majority of college students are broke.

We all fall victim to thinking about the now instead of planning for the future. My friends that turned to that life are not happy. They still talk about pursuing their goals but feel stuck because they have to keep up with the lifestyle they now have. When you start living a lifestyle that is glamorous (to the human eye), more than likely, it will be hard to break away from what kept you in that lifestyle. The car, rent, clothes, etc. still have to be paid for, so making a sacrifice to go all in toward a goal that may not produce "fast cash" may put you back a bit, which is why those who usually choose the fast route first never really reach their goals. This doesn't mean it isn't possible, but it is hard and will take a lot of changing your life around. All things are definitely possible, but we want to learn from others' mistakes, right? Everything that glitters is not gold, and anything worth having is worth fighting for.

Again, am I serious? Yes, I am! We all become vulnerable when life gets rough. If I have more positive people (those who are willing to work and sacrifice, and who have discipline and determination), than those looking for an easy way out around me during those times, I'm less likely to go down the wrong path. Their motivation helps me to endure, to move forward!

Remember, it takes missing one deadline to miss out on admission or money for college, and it takes one skipped class to turn into two, three, or more, which can lead to an F in a class. Each class prepares you for the next, so if you fall behind, it's going to take much more work to catch up. Most teenagers enter one of these scenarios due to hanging out with "friends" whose goals don't align with theirs.

How do you add someone to your community? Ask your advisors at school or church, ask a librarian, or browse the internet for local clubs or organizations that may be of interest to you. Join one or two. Typically, students who join clubs or organizations outside of class all have something in common. They all want to do more than what is required to achieve a goal (i.e. joining a club). I'm sure you will click with many people there and hopefully become friends.

STRETCH

So, let's see who is in your community. Write them here:

Mentors:

Friends:

Family:

Do you need to remove anyone or distance yourself? List the names of the people you may need to create distance from here:

My friends started going down a path that I didn't feel was promising. I knew I needed to distance myself from them, but we are still able to be cordial with each other. Start changing for the better, and if your friend that always ends up in trouble starts to make changes because you have, then encourage them. We are never better than anyone else, we just want something different for ourselves. When the people around us want better, then we must help them as well.

Sometimes you may be called names like disloyal or fake when you make a decision to stop hanging with the wrong crowd or going to bad places. Trust me, I've been there, and I can guarantee you it was worth it. Plus, if they are really your friends, they won't mind spending less time with you so you can get your life together. You don't have to announce to them that you are not going to hang out as much. Just let them know you have to do homework, stay after class, go to the store, or anything until the time apart is normal. They are either going to want to start doing better, too, or they'll remain doing the opposite. The choice for you is yours, and the choice for them is theirs.

Whew! By this time, we have talked about and done a lot! Let's see how much we have stretched:

1. We have realized that our circumstances do not define us. Our circumstances make us stronger and motivate us to work twice as hard to change our futures.
2. We acknowledged that we may have to fight a little harder, but we're not going to make excuses.
3. We know that we can't wait for handouts because more than likely, we won't get them.
4. We understand that we are in control of our future.
5. Although things may seem unfair, we cannot be reborn in a different circumstance or wait for a fair life to reach us.
6. We have found motivation through the negative and positive events in our lives.
7. We understand that we must decide in our MINDS that we can rise above our doubts or others' doubts about us.
8. We found motivation in the possibility of living a greater life later.
9. We acknowledge that this may not be easy but worth it.
10. We have set up our community of supporters because we know times may get rough, and we need them to continue to not only push us forward, but also assist us with our journey.

STRETCH

You may be thinking, what does this have to do with college? Well, most successful college students do all of the above daily to maintain good grades, graduate (with less debt), and gain great employment after college. The bottom line is that great students recognize that just going to class isn't enough. So, go back and reread the points that challenge you the most. Keep in mind that when you stretch, you are stretching to become comfortable (successful). Most times, you may have to do something you have never done to get something you've never had!

Are you ready to move forward? We are now ready to practice the five Ps.

Proper Planning Prevents Poor Performance.

Go ahead and say it aloud:

 **Proper.**
Planning.
Prevents.
Poor.
Performance.

Memorize it.
Understand it.
DO IT!!

"I doubt performing poorly is a part of the plan!"

The key words in this common saying are proper and planning. What does it mean to be proper? It means that you are doing things appropriately.

STRETCH

You may plan to attend a wedding and wear whatever you choose. However, the invitation asks for after-five attire. Showing up in a jogging suit shows you planned to attend because you showed up, but arriving in a nice suit would show that you PROPERLY planned.

Why should you properly plan?

Benjamin Franklin coined the phrase that is quite simple yet profound: When you fail to plan, you plan to fail. Waiting on a mysterious amount of money, a person, or thing to save you will result in you waiting your entire life. Don't let life pass you by, by allowing your dreams to remain just that, dreams. Planning causes you to focus on a goal and produce results.

Take owning a salon, for example. You want to own a salon, so you begin planning. You research the necessary education required, when you're going to apply, and when you should be finished, for starters. It is almost impossible to pass up a deadline after you plan to apply. Since it is a part of your plan, you begin to take the necessary steps to complete the application process. When you plan, it reduces the possible setbacks, roadblocks, or unwanted changes. Some situations are inevitable; however, when you plan properly, you identify possible setbacks.

While planning to apply for school, you notice that the time of one of the mandatory courses interferes with your job. Since you planned ahead of time, you

STRETCH

were able to check with an advisor to see if the schedule will remain the same the following year. You may also make arrangements with your job to switch your hours in time for the first day of class.

Since you have planned properly, even the setbacks you didn't identify shouldn't stop you. Your knowledge and practice of proper planning should help you to replan around whatever curveball life throws at you. Proper planning helps to give you direction. What you do in and out of school now serves a purpose. You understand that the decisions you make can ultimately keep you on track or cause you to fall off. When you have direction, you are basically bridging together the gap of where you are and where you want to go. Everything you do has a purpose, and you are no longer drifting, waiting for opportunity to hit you. You are planning your future; doesn't it look bright?!

I know too well how hard it is to picture yourself living a better life when low self-esteem, peer pressure, and negative things surround you. Trust me when I say that when you properly plan, you begin to spark a fire in your imagination that helps you to become creative and ultimately shift your way of thinking to where you see multiple positive outcomes. All it takes is a pen and a piece of paper.

Let's look at how this works. Your plan is to become a beautician and shop owner. You begin to plan by reaching out to job shadow a stylist. You see her styling a wig for a cancer patient. This sparks your interest, and you begin to see yourself helping cancer patients as well, specifically children. This leads you to research local children's hospitals to volunteer. While volunteering, you see a need for a beauty shop within the hospital where children may come to get wigs and play dress-up. This leads you to begin planning to get a degree in business alongside your cosmetology license.

You see what just happened? When you begin to plan your future and take action (even if it is just one step) and when you do not allow circumstances to cloud your vision, you begin to allow creativity to enter in. The next thing you know, you are moving in a direction that you could have never dreamed about before.

In college, when Plan A didn't work, I went back to the drawing board to come up with a Plan B. My goal didn't change, just my approach! Since my problem with school has always been money (I didn't properly plan before entering), I could have easily been too discouraged to continue. But once you start the habit of properly planning, it helps you to think positively. Constantly planning helps to awaken the creative juices within you. It helps you to move forward and become more strategic. You may ask your community to assist you in planning (besides, we're not all experts in everything), but whatever you do, continue to plan.

Let's review. When you plan you:

Seeking expert advice is important. Many students have problems with the college-going process simply because they fail to ask questions. Every step of the way, you should ask questions, even if you think you know what you are talking about. Even if you may not have questions or don't know what to ask, sit down with your school's career or college counselor or mentor and tell them your plans or ideas. They should be able to assist you with strengthening your approach.

EXAMPLE

When college admission is the ultimate goal, you must create a list of "mini" goals that will place you closer to your destination. Your list of goals may look different than your peers' depending on where you are. You may have to explore careers before doing anything else. Whatever you do, work on a date that you would want to complete your ultimate goal (applying for admission into college) by. Then fill up the calendar in between now and that time with your mini goals that will assist you with applying.

STRETCH

A goal without a plan is just a dream! Consider some of the following:

- Reading books not assigned in class
- Joining a club
- Getting a mentor
- Researching / applying for scholarships
- Going on a college tour
- Volunteering
- Raising grades
- Researching careers / Job Shadowing

Doing any of these will help you to discover cool things about yourself that will assist you with properly planning your life after high school.

? Write down a plan to achieve each step toward your goal with deadlines.

Goal	To-Do's	Deadline

? Identify possible barriers.

Goal	Barriers

? Identify possible routes around the barriers. Talk to advisors and mentors about your concerns and ways to overcome them. Ask if what you think is a barrier is a real barrier. Sometimes we think negatively before thinking positively. This leads us to create our own barriers by allowing them to guide our decisions, so ASK just in case the solution may be in arm's reach. It may be just an ant to a giant.

Goal	Barrier	Routes Around Barrier(s)

* If you need to, but don't give up on the goal.

"When you constantly plan, you are less likely to perform poorly, because I doubt performing poorly is a part of the plan."

Ready, Set, Go!

Preparing for your life after high school begins today. There are many routes one may choose to take, such as the Armed Forces (Army, Navy, Marines, etc.), Job Corps, and workforce. Fortunately, all of the lessons taught in this book can be transferred to help you make the best decision for you. I'm a firm believer in higher education, whether it is getting certified in a skill or going for a doctorate degree. No matter the time requirements, it is important that one continues to better oneself, not only for a paycheck, but also to improve their overall quality of life. The discipline you learn and use to complete a degree program is the same discipline you can transfer to other areas of your life. Since I made almost every mistake possible while trying to navigate the college-going process, I hope I can use what I have learned from those mistakes to inspire and prevent you from making the same mistakes.

Gap year—If you're like me, you may not have begun thinking about college until your senior year. Or you just may not know what you want to go to school for.

STRETCH

Some students choose to take a year off to explore before starting college. This does not mean that you get a year off to do nothing. This means you are actively researching careers, job shadowing, networking, visiting schools, reading more, and exploring your gifts, talents, and passion. It is never wise to jump into school just because your peers are going. College costs, so make sure you properly plan before starting.

So, what do you want to be when you grow up? Pause. Before you answer, eliminate all negative thoughts. You can do it!

? Now, what do you want to be as an adult?

? What are your plans to start moving toward your goal? Don't forget to share your goal and possible plan with your mentor. If you have a goal but don't know where to begin, make sure you seek advice from your community.

? What are your concerns? (Finances? Support? Time?)

Not sure what you want to do? Keep reading, I may be able to help you. Just make sure you come back to the question once it hits you.

My Slow Start

In high school, I had a 1.8 cumulative GPA. I really struggled with my classwork. It wasn't until I heard my friends discussing their goals and which colleges they were going to apply to that I began to take my coursework seriously. I paid attention to not only the subject I was good at, but also what I enjoyed learning about. I enjoyed biology, so I began to ask myself the same question that I asked you: What do I want to be when I grow up?

Dentistry

Growing up, my mom would never smile. Her teeth weren't white, straight, or shiny, so she refrained from smiling because of it. I thought it was awful to want to smile, but to feel so overwhelmed by the appearance of her teeth that she didn't do it. Since my mom didn't have dental insurance as a child, she was left with less attractive teeth in her adult years. I wanted to be a dentist because I enjoyed biology, and I had a cause behind it. I wanted to be a dentist to help those who didn't have dental insurance.

Are you passionate about something? Do you want to change something? Combining your strengths and passions is a great way to discover what you would like to do after high school. Write them here.

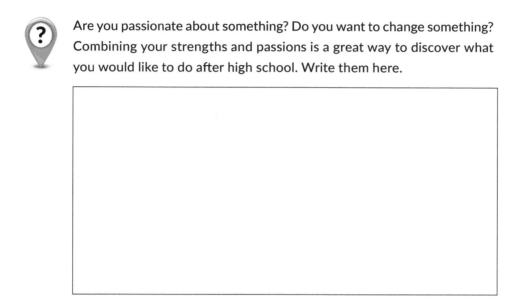

After I figured out that I wanted to be a dentist, I had to figure out how to get there. Well, the first thing I had to do was turn my grades around. To become a dentist, I had to go to college, but in order for me to get into college, I had to prove that I could do college work. I knew this because I began to research by typing "How to become a dentist" in the search engine on the world wide web (internet). I found that I needed eight years of schooling after high school.

I didn't look at my grades and think, impossible. I looked at my grades and said, "I have some work to do."

That is exactly what I did. I worked hard by staying after class every day until I understood the material. I truly thought it was never too late to start fresh, and I was right—it wasn't!

Reality

Do you think I could have attempted to pursue a challenging career with a 1.8 cumulative GPA? I had a lot of nerve! I mean, confidence! You have to believe in yourself no matter what. At the same time, you have to be realistic. My late start trying to get good grades pointed me in the right direction to achieving my goal of becoming a dentist. However, realistically, it was too late for me to get into a four-year college. I received rejection letter after rejection letter. I guess I should have given up then, right? I mean, my grades had gone from horrible to mediocre. The only thing I had was this fire inside of me wanting a better life for myself. This fire or desire didn't go out even when I received not one, not two, but three rejection letters from colleges I had applied to. I believed in myself when it seemed like no one else did.

?

Do you believe in yourself? What are you doing to show that you believe in yourself?

Since I was still determined, I allowed my rejection to fuel my imagination. I began to think outside of the box. Although I saw most of my friends go to big universities and move into their dorms, I knew what I had to do. I couldn't get jealous of them or quit. I had to find an alternate route to my goal, and that route was community college. By the way, I didn't have help from my guidance counselor in high school. I guess since I didn't look good on paper, they didn't see college in my future. But I did, and that is all that mattered!

Community College

Being accepted into a community college is much easier than a four-year college or university. In most cases, simply applying for entry will get you accepted.

 What community colleges are in your area? List them below:
(A simple search on the world wide web will do. Also, don't forget to ask your school advisor for assistance.)

I chose to attend the Milwaukee Area Technical College to take college-level courses. My plan was to transfer to a four-year college because the career I researched required a bachelor's degree and that is a degree you can't obtain at a community college. I knew at the time that I wanted to be a dentist, so I decided to enroll in a program that had the word *dental* in it: Dental Technology. After one year, I completed the program and received my diploma in Dental Technology.

After I graduated from MATC, I applied to Alverno College. I had finally received my first acceptance letter into a four-year college. My plan worked! I attended community college to show that I could get great grades, worked hard, and never gave up, and now I had an opportunity to achieve my dreams. I thought that everything was going smoothly, until I found out that graduating from the Dental Technology program wasn't a good idea. Going to community college was a good idea, but what I studied was not.

To some it may be viewed as a good idea, but to others, it was a waste of time. Keep in mind that my saying the decisions I made were either good or bad for ME was because it was based upon MY plan. Enrolling in a certificate program at a community college may be a good idea for YOU, if it is a part of your PLAN.

Let's explore both sides. Bad decision (for me): Since I knew I would be applying into a four-year program, I should have taken what are called general education courses. General education courses are required by all students who want to obtain a bachelor's degree. These courses are usually math, science, social science, and English. If I would have taken these types of courses while at the community college, I would have entered the four-year college as a sophomore. I entered as a freshman because the classes I took for the Dental Technology program were specific to that career and geared toward me going to work after graduation and not back to school.

At community colleges, you have several options. You can take classes that will transfer to a college or university, you can use your classes for professional development, you can take classes for fun, or you can take classes that will prepare you for a specific job after you graduate. If you choose to take classes that prepare you for a job immediately following graduation, it's most likely that your credits will not transfer to a four-year school (since a four-year degree isn't required for that specific career).

Just as you wouldn't expect to get a bachelor's degree from a community college, you shouldn't expect to get a cosmetology certificate from a four-year college or university. This is why you must brainstorm, plan, and meet with academic advisors to make sure you are making the right decisions for you. If I would have met with an advisor and told them my goals, I'm sure they would have made sure that I didn't enroll in the Dental Technology program. It was a waste of time and money for ME!

Good decision: On the other hand, my decision to graduate with a diploma in Dental Technology may seem like a good idea to others. The job market may be tough for those without any post-secondary (after high school) education and experience. By completing a program like Dental Technology, Dental Assisting, Nursing Assistant, Cosmetology, or any other one-to-two-year programs that do not require a lot of time in school, you may increase your chances of employment. If you need to work while in school like I had to, this route may work. With a diploma, certificate, or degree, you become more marketable. If you plan on attending a four-year school, be aware that these courses may not transfer, but earning money while in school, especially if you don't have much financial help, may not be a horrible idea. Obtaining a diploma or technical degree not only opens up a way to make money, but it looks really good on a résumé.

(A résumé is a document used to display your skills, education, and employment background.)

After obtaining a bachelor's degree, I planned on applying to dental school. With both programs on my résumé, I'm sure my application would have looked more appealing to those reviewing my application for admission than someone who didn't have any dental experience on their résumé.

Using other areas, let's look at other possible ways my option to attend community college was a good idea.

Scenario #1: Student didn't perform well in high school but wants to be a nurse.

Barrier: Student applies to the nursing program at a community college, but due to their past grades, they don't get in.

Nursing and dental hygiene programs are competitive to get into, even at the community college level. A lot of the coursework associated with these programs may transfer to four-year schools, because they require some general education classes. Completion of these programs will grant you an associate's degree.

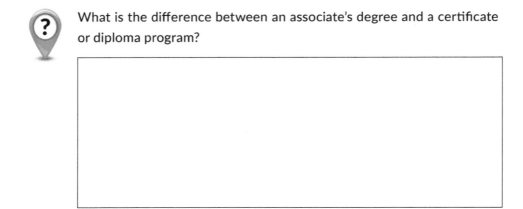

What is the difference between an associate's degree and a certificate or diploma program?

My program was a diploma program, so all my courses were like on-the-job training and it only took one year to complete. An associate's degree typically takes two years to complete, and within that program you take classes that are transferable, and you may be able to pursue employment with it as well.

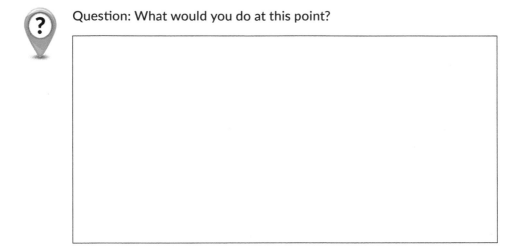

Question: What would you do at this point?

Possible solution (but there are more): There are many answers to a problem, but the wrong answer would be to give up! Typically, when life throws you lemons, rejection, disappointment, or barriers, this is when you should allow the pressure from those circumstances to push you to a higher level of thinking. Be creative, innovative, and inspired. When you do, you can't lose. The most triumphant stories come after tragedy. Keep pushing, and don't forget to keep PROPERLY PLANNING!

The student may enroll in a Medical Assisting or Certified Nursing (CNA) program instead. They know these classes may not transfer to a four-year college, as they plan to apply for jobs upon graduation in their field. This will give them a chance to improve their grades and give them experience. The completion of the program may increase the student's chances of gaining entry into the nursing program once they reapply for entry. Now that the student is working for a hospital or clinic, they may find that their employer may pay for their education if they continue on the nursing or medical career path.

Hint: This student must have identified "funding" as a POSSIBLE barrier to their goal since their REPLAN incorporated a solution for it.

A lot of medical clinics and hospitals will pay for you to go back to school. You will only know what is out there if you ask questions and do research. Do not be afraid, you got this! This is one scenario out of many different possibilities. The student could have taken general education courses, then transferred to a four-year college to pursue a bachelor's in nursing as opposed to an associate nursing degree (two years) from a community college.

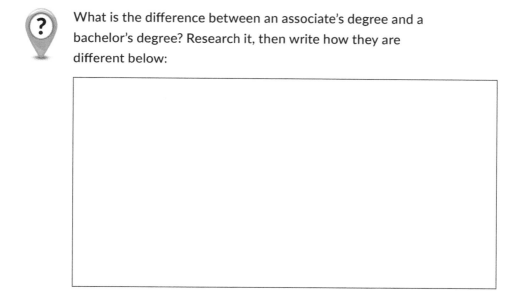

? What is the difference between an associate's degree and a bachelor's degree? Research it, then write how they are different below:

Now, let's explore the same scenario we used to illustrate proper planning.

Scenario #2: You, the student, love children. You love them so much that you want to become a licensed daycare owner. You begin shadowing a daycare teacher before making your decision on college choices (Hint: Job shadowing is effective to help you in your college decision and field of study decision). After job shadowing, your mentor allows you to become the "daycare attendant." You are now doing feedings, reading, and playtime with the children. You are gaining experience and earning some money. Even if you didn't earn any money, you would (should) be satisfied with the experience.

 **Most internships or job shadowing do not have a financial return; however, they give you something that money cannot buy—experience, networking, and a sound mind by knowing if you want to continue on that career path or not.**

 List Possible places/people to job shadow below:

-
-
-

STRETCH
While in high school, if you find that you are interested in a career, you should ask your school counselor or mentor to help identify someone in that field for you to study. You may also, on your own, search the internet, and reach out to possible people working in your community who have the career you're interested in shadowing. Shadowing before you go to college is a smart idea. You can literally determine if a career is for you before putting time and money into college.

Name (Contact or Organization)	Telephone # or Email	Address	Possible Barriers (Ex: Time, transportation, etc.)	Routes Around Barriers

Job shadowing has really helped you to make your decision about becoming a daycare owner. You then apply to the community college in your area because you found out, after doing research, that this profession does not require a four-year bachelor's degree. By now, working at the daycare helps you to envision yourself starting your own company. Placing yourself in this new role has caused your mind to wander. You begin to envision how you can make your career your own by mixing the two things you love: children and being a business owner.

As you begin to actively think about how to make your passion for business and children (coupled with life experience) all come together to guide your education process, you allow your mind to think outside the box. From this point on, you could attend community college to obtain your daycare license while taking business courses to obtain an associate's in business. Or you could take general education courses that will enable you to transfer to a four-year college to obtain your bachelor's degree in business or education. After you receive your daycare license and business degree, you are equipped with the knowledge to pitch a business proposal.

Whenever your goals include receiving multiple degrees or transferring colleges, it is imperative that you not only discuss your plan with an academic

STRETCH

advisor at the college you plan on enrolling in, but with a financial aid counselor as well. Here is a financial preview (the financial aid section is coming soon). Financial aid is NOT everlasting. It does cut off. You cannot stay in school forever and expect assistance. To make sure your plans align with financial aid limits, please ALWAYS consult a financial aid officer. As always, if you need assistance with asking questions, ask your mentor or school counselor to do a conference call with the school so they can assist you with what you miss.

In addition to learning about the vast opportunities for learning at community colleges, hopefully what you saw in the scenario above is the importance of putting yourself out there by job shadowing. When we open ourselves up to new possibilities, experiences, and people, we create a perfect arena for dreams to take place that we would have never dreamed of. When you allow yourself to be innovative and excited about your future, action has to take place. Allow your actions (making plans, asking questions, doing research) to move you into a world of unknown possibilities.

(?) What are your hobbies?

(?) What moves/motivates you?

? What are you good at?

? What are you not good at but willing to work hard toward to fulfill your dreams and goals?

I may not be good in math, but because it is required in my nursing program, I'm going to work hard (tutoring, peer study groups, etc.) to do well because I know doing well in that subject will place me closer to my dreams.

Four-Year Colleges/ Universities

After I graduated from the Milwaukee Area Technical College with my Dental Technology diploma, I decided to apply to a four-year school. I needed to go to a four-year school to earn a bachelor's degree if I wanted to go to dental school. I knew that because I researched my dream job and what it took for me to get there. Unlike the first time I applied to four-year schools, I was admitted because I was able to prove that I could get good grades when I attended the community college. With my dream job of being a dentist as my focus, I decided to major in biology and minor in chemistry.

? What does it mean to major in a subject?

? What does it mean to minor in a subject?

? Why would you major or minor in a subject?

I chose those subjects because after I researched "how to become a dentist," I found that I would have to apply to dental school after receiving my bachelor's degree. Dental schools require a test to gain entrance into their school, called the DAT. This test is comprised of math and science. Also, some dental schools require science prerequisites.

Prerequisites are classes that must be completed in order to move on to the next class or level.

I could have majored in anything, as long as I made sure to take all the prerequisites while in my four-year school. But since I enjoyed science, I was killing two birds with one stone. Researching my dream profession helped me tremendously, but speaking with academic advisors at the college helped me to determine if I was making the right choices.

If I could have started off my college career at a four-year school, I would have. My high school grades didn't afford me that option, but I did eventually go! College is about more than gaining a degree. Gaining a degree is important, but the experience you gain, new friends you meet, and life skills you accrue are something to be considered when deciding which path you should take. I always wanted to attend a big college with football and basketball teams so I could play in the band. I admired how people went back to their colleges after they graduated for homecoming. Unfortunately, I didn't attend a four-year school that met all of my desires. I attended a small, four-year, private all-girls school simply because it's where my sister attended.

Following friends, boyfriends/girlfriends, or family members to school is not the best way to decide which option is best for YOU.

I began my time at Alverno College, but I was so unhappy that I ended up transferring from there to a big four-year public school in Chicago, The University of Illinois at Chicago. I will get into how transferring schools was such a huge financial headache later on in the book, but for now it is important that you do some research. First, I will go over the different types of schools by comparing community colleges to four-year schools. It is up to you to decide which route is the best to take.

Here are a few routes you may take from high school to college:

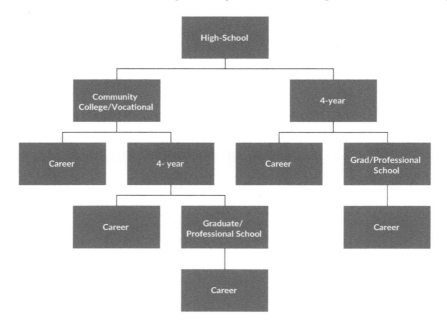

What are the differences between four-year college and community colleges?

	Community College	4-year College or University
Purpose	Workforce training, hobbies, general education	Well-rounded education that prepares you for not only employment, but social involvement, and graduate/professional school.
Degrees	Diploma, certificate, and associate	Bachelor
Entrance	Open enrollment	Contingent upon prior coursework, test scores, essays, and involvement
Housing	Typically no, but some offer housing	Yes
Time	Typically 1-2 years	Typically 4 years
Ages	Varies	18-22 (Typically)
Cost	Less expensive (before financial aid)	More expensive (before financial aid)
Extracurricular/Campus Life	Clubs and some sports teams *Since a lot of students may be nontraditional or commuters (don't reside on campus), the campus life may not be as robust.	Clubs and sport teams, sororities and fraternities *Both types of schools offer extracurricular activities; however, you may have more to choose from at a four-year school with more students being involved.

If you are only interested in a community college for the size, keep in mind that not all four-year colleges are huge. You may want to explore some smaller colleges in addition to some larger ones when you plan your search.

When considering which school to attend, here are some questions you may want to ask:

1. *Does my career require an associate's or bachelor's degree?*

2. *Which pathway is best for me?*
   Is your academic performance good enough to begin at a four-year school? If not, does the four-year school offer what are typically referred to as Bridge Programs? Bridge Programs are an opportunity to take classes that are worth zero credits and/or are free of charge. The programs are typically offered during the summer. They allow you to bridge the gap between your high school GPA and college acceptance. This way, when you start your first semester, you will be ready to begin taking classes that will count toward your degree. Some four-year schools will give you a chance, so don't count them out if you didn't perform well in high school. Apply and ask to see if the school offers such ways to get you where you need to be.

3. *Do you have to work and attend school?*
   This is a reality for many students. They must consider many different variables when making a decision on schools. Just make sure the school choice allows you to progress toward your degree in a timely manner.

Make sure you come up with a work plan that goes with your school plan. Tell your advisors what your circumstance is so everyone involved can help you reach your goal. It is VERY important to communicate your circumstance to your academic advisor and financial aid advisor at the school, because you want to make sure your school schedule makes it easier for you to work, and also that you will complete your degree in a timely manner. Remember, financial aid does run out, so make sure you are transparent.

STRETCH

4. *Does the school offer the extracurricular activities you are interested in?*
   College is a place where you go to do well academically, but it is also a place where you can really explore clubs, cheer for a team, join a sorority or fraternity, etc. I wish I would have attended a school that had a football team and a homecoming. The experiences my friends had and continue to have, even after graduating, are experiences that I truly missed out on.

5. *Will you need to attend online classes?*
   I believe students get more from being in the classroom, but if you need to have this option available to you, make sure the school has a lot of support/advising accessible to you.

6. *Does the school you're interested in offer the major you would like to study? If so, the next important question is whether the school is accredited.*

    Accreditation is when a school is recognized to be qualified to teach or grant a degree in a particular field. Not only does the school need to be accredited, but the program within the school that you're in needs to be accredited. If the school is not, then you risk graduating and your degree not being seen as official. I've seen students go to schools that were not accredited and graduate, but then they couldn't move forward within their field because the employer would not accept their degree. What a waste of time and money! It is important that you research and ask the schools about their accreditation.

7. *For-profit vs. Nonprofit*

    As a financial aid officer, I see a lot of students who attend for-profit schools and come out with a lot of debt and degrees that are not accredited. Typically, they offer a lot of courses that are pleasing to the older and working student. The problem is that some cannot offer the same amount of gift/free money to its students, so you may be able to attend a four-year nonprofit or community college for much less. Also, I've seen, especially when students want to gain a medical assistant, nursing, CNA, or non-bachelor-degree required medical certificate, schools that "specialize" in that training and pass a lot of students, but the students are not passing their boards (required state exam that most healthcare providers must pass in order to work in their field). We call these places diploma mills because they make it easy to pass their classes (graduating students), however, the students are not prepared to take the state exam to get a job in healthcare. They are simply taking money from students. It is a big scam.

8. *Do you prefer a big school or a small school?*
   The only way to really know what school is for you is to visit. Most high schools allow their students time off to attend colleges. Others may use their holiday time off, but keep in mind if you're out of school, then most college students are as well.

Below, make a list of schools you would like to visit and when. Visiting prior to your senior year of high school is highly suggested. Try to select a private, public, and a community college so you can compare. If you have the option, try to visit big vs. small schools, as well as historically black colleges and universities outside your state of residence.

School Name	Date of Anticipated Visit

STRETCH

Visiting Colleges can get expensive, so consider the following:

- Start close to home

- Plan with friends

- See if the college has any way to reduce the cost (fly-in programs)

- Ask your school counselor about any school tours

- Take virtual tours via YouTube, read student blogs, and follow Facebook and Twitter accounts

*Do not skip this step. Visiting and researching schools is important. It will assist you with choosing the school that is the best fit for you! If you are having a hard time finding various schools, please refer to www. Collegeboard.org. They have a great college search tool that will help you develop a great list of schools.

When you take a campus visit, make sure that you observe the following:

School Type and Name	Class/ Campus Size (Like/Dislike)	Professors (Approachable?)	Clubs/Sports and Tutor Programs (Offers different ways to get help with work)	Dorm/ Food	Admissions/ Financial Aid (Approachable? Knowledgeable?)	Career Center? Default Rate (low) Employment (high)
1.						
2.						
3.						
4.						
5.						
6.						
7.						
8.						

Since I didn't perform well in high school, my counselor didn't provide me with options, because he didn't think college was for me. During your research, be careful not to allow someone else's perception of you and your capabilities to deter you from your dream. If someone tells you that community college is your only option, make sure you research more options like the Bridge Programs mentioned earlier (I've seen some called Chance as well). Continue to seek advice from those who can provide you with many solutions/routes other than a boxed-in viewpoint! It's your life, begin to create it.

My process for gaining my bachelor's degree was complete trial and error. Luckily, I made enough right decisions that led me to a degree, but it was very costly. Cost! The reason why I am writing this book is because of the decisions I made that cost me a lot of money. When I transferred to the University of Illinois at Chicago after my second year at Alverno, I thought I made the right decision, but financially I didn't. Now we must jump into a component that should help you decide which route works best for you and your family: price.

"Yes! I've been accepted into college, but show me the money."

Show Me the Money/ Financial Aid

Money, or the lack of, is what many students use to determine their educational paths. Many times, the decisions that are being made are based upon passed down myths regarding the financial aid process. I, on the other hand, did not think about the money piece at all. I was not concerned with the bill or how it was getting paid. I thought I was doing what was right by going to school. I thought, like many other college students, that financial aid paid for everything. I was totally wrong.

As a financial aid officer, the problem that I see is that many families do not understand how financial aid works. I see many students who do well academically but can't continue due to outstanding balances that stem from their misconception of the financial aid process. Financial aid varies from state to state. I probably made every possible financial mistake and now, as a financial aid officer, I plan on using what I learned to assist you with one of the main reasons students from various backgrounds do not graduate: the misconception of financial aid.

Now that you have some idea of what you would like to do, the next step is understanding how to pay for it. We will begin by going over the financial aid process.

What is financial aid? Financial aid may be in the form of grants (given based upon level of need), scholarships (typically based upon grades), and loans (you will have to pay back).

Grants *Based upon need *Apply by completing a FAFSA	Scholarships *Based upon merit
Loans *Federal Loans *Apply by completing a FAFSA	Work Study *Based upon need *Apply by completing a FAFSA

Separate from your scholarship search, most schools require that you complete a Free Application for Federal Student Aid (FAFSA) to see if you are eligible for any state, federal, or institutional grants. The application should be completed as soon as possible beginning October 1st of your senior year in high school. Some schools may require additional applications, so make sure you give them a call and ask what is needed to begin the financial aid process at that school. To illustrate how important it is to complete your FAFSA sooner rather than later, I'll use the State of Illinois MAP Grant as an example. The Illinois MAP Grant is given to students who have need (demonstrated by the FAFSA), who are Illinois residents and attend an Illinois school (most state grants are only given to residents of that state who remain in-state for school), and students who complete the FAFSA before the MAP deadline date. The key is that the public does not know when that date is, because the grant is given on a first come, first served basis. Once funding is gone, even if you are eligible based upon your FAFSA results and residency, you miss out on gift aid (money that doesn't have to be paid back) due to a timing issue. When you complete your FAFSA early, you are basically saving your spot in line so that, if you are eligible for grants, you will indeed receive them. Also, keep in mind that your name, social security number, and date of birth must be correct when you submit and successfully sign the initial FAFSA. If any of these things are incorrect (the information that identifies you as you), then your spot is not saved.

When I was applying for college, I allowed the price of the school to determine if I should apply or not. Yes, some or possibly most students make their education decision based upon price, but I'm here to let you know that that is a big mistake during the application process. The reason is because when you look at a school's website, it gives you the amount for tuition and fees. If you plan on staying on campus, you'll also see costs for room and board (and food/meal plan). This is what I like to call sticker prices. This price is what it will cost before financial aid is applied. Since you have to apply for college admission before you complete your FAFSA, you will not know what it will actually cost you until after you apply for FAFSA and receive your award package from all the schools you listed on your FAFSA.

I have seen students attend a community college before applying to a four-year school because they thought it was cheaper. Sometimes four-year schools offer larger scholarships to incoming freshmen students than transfers. This is why I encourage students to apply to various types of schools. I'll break down what I mean by "various" here:

Reach schools. These are the schools that seem out of reach academically and financially. Typically, these are your four-year private schools. Oftentimes, these types of schools may have additional funds to provide students. They also may offer summer courses before your first year begins to prep you for the year to come. If your dream school is considered a reach school for you, apply and make sure you talk to a financial aid counselor and academic counselor at the school to share your concerns so the professionals can assist you with resources that may be available to help you succeed. You have to speak up. Keep in mind that sometimes these discussions will illustrate that the school you wanted to attend may not be a good fit for you. You may want to attend your reach school, but it is safe and wise to apply to a few "safety" schools.

Safety schools. Safety schools are the schools you know for a fact that you meet the grade point average (GPA) required for entry and whose sticker price is less than the reach schools. The safety schools are typically your public four-year schools.

Guaranteed school. Lastly, I always recommend that students apply to a guaranteed school, A.K.A. a local community college. Even if your end goal is a four-year degree, as I said previously, you can start there and then transfer. Sometimes your plans fall through; it is always safe to have a backup plan.

The key is to have options. If you plan on applying to all out-of-state schools, keep in mind that most out-of-state schools charge students who are not from that state more money. This doesn't mean you shouldn't apply. This means you should apply for some in-state options as well so you have something to compare it to. Subsequently, if you properly plan, you may find that some states have tuition reciprocity programs that allow students from a neighboring state to attend their state schools and vice versa at a discounted or in-state tuition rate.

STRETCH

I worked with a student who only applied to one school. Academically, he met the requirements, but financially, his family could not come up with the amount that financial aid did not cover. Since most application deadlines are before you receive your financial aid results, by the time he figured out that he couldn't attend his dream school, it was too late to apply to any other four-year school. He could apply to his community college, as most have flexible enrollment. Keep in mind, life is more stressful when you do things this way. You may find yourself rushing to get enrolled, and that's not a good feeling when you're entering a new/unfamiliar part of your life. In this case, he still had an option, just not his preferred second option!

List two schools of each below that you're interested in and that have your intended area of study:

Type of School	In-State	Out-of-State
Reach		
Safety		
Guaranteed		

I did not apply to multiple schools. I applied to the school my sister went to because it was easy. I didn't have to do research on a school that my sister went to because she had already gone through the process. The problem was that she had a huge scholarship and her room and board was paid for. I did not have a huge scholarship, so when I went, I applied for private student loans. I would ask their financial aid counselors about the aid process, but it was never explained how everything worked. If I had been counseled correctly, I probably could have transferred out of the school before getting myself in so much debt.

Without wise counseling to help me understand how financial aid worked, I repeated my mistake and only applied to one school to transfer to. When I transferred to the big four-year school in Chicago, I ended up changing my major, which meant I would have to be in school longer. This seemed fine, until I found out that financial aid has limits.

A common misconception is that financial aid will be an option until you graduate. To not confuse you, just know – before you transfer schools or come up with a plan to begin at a community college and transfer, or get one degree then go back for another like we went over in the community college section of this book – discuss what your plans are with a financial aid counselor. Ask them if the time you are in school matches with your financial aid limits. Ask one counselor and then verify the answer with another counselor. Yes, it is that serious!

When students go to the financial aid office knowing their potential problems, plans, or some financial aid knowledge, the counselor has more material to

STRETCH

assist them with. Financial aid is a complex field, so how it may work for one student may not apply to you. This is why it is best to not go off of word-of-mouth but by the information you obtain yourself through one-on-one counseling visits. Keep in mind that you should ask each school you are applying to the same questions. What works at one school may not be the case at another. Your school may have counselors that talk to you or have people come in to talk about financial aid to you and your classmates. They may give you general information about financial aid, but what you want is specifics. The only way to get that type of information is to call each school you are considering.

Before we dive into what the FAFSA has to offer, let's look into scholarships. Another reason why I believe it is never too early to begin looking into what you would like to do after graduation is because the majority of the time, proper and timely planning leads to more scholarships. After you decide that you would like to go to college, you should begin to not only look at the requirements it takes to get into your school of choice, but also if they offer scholarships. Most school websites have a scholarship section. Many are hard to find. Trust me, I've tried looking for them with my students. If you can't find the section, give the school a call. Do not quit because of frustration.

Attempt to get navigation help from the school. What you will find once you locate the scholarship portion is that some schools automatically award scholarships based upon your high school grades and testing scores. Some schools will admit you without considering your ACT or SAT scores. They are test optional. If those schools use your test scores to determine scholarship eligibility, then when you apply to get into school, do NOT choose the "test optional" option. If you do not provide your ACT or SAT scores at a school that uses that information for their merit scholarships, then you will not be considered for them. So, make sure to call the school to get clarity on what they use to award their scholarships.

HINT: If you didn't perform well on the ACT or SAT, you may not want to include your scores. Please consider how your scores will or will not increase your chances of admission and additional financial aid before making a decision.

Others may require that you complete an application. Some will outline their requirements, others may not. Unfortunately, some websites are harder to navigate than others, however, that is still not an excuse. If you're unable to find the information you need, please pick up the phone and give the Financial Aid or Admissions Office a call. Who awards scholarships at each school may vary, but Financial Aid and Admissions Offices are the best places to start with when asking questions.

Ultimately, as a student, you should always try to get good grades and make the most out of your high school experience. When you join clubs, you are creating an environment where you learn how to run a club, network, and gain skills that are great for any type of application (job, school, scholarships). Most schools offer scholarships; however, you should also apply for external scholarships. These are scholarships that are outside of your potential college. Your club, school, local legislators, and businesses in your community may offer scholarship options. Your guidance counselor may know about some of these, but you should be prepared to do your own research as well. The only way to get an answer is to ask questions. Don't be afraid to look into all your options. For example, if there is a McDonald's in your area, don't hesitate to go online and research what scholarships they may offer.

I was working with a student who had scored a 23 on his ACT. After researching the school that he wanted to attend, we found that he could have half of his tuition covered if

STRETCH

he had a 24 or higher on his ACT. At the time, he was satisfied with his score and had no plans to retake it. However, since we had discovered this his junior year, he was able to study and retake the ACT to try to get the 24 or higher before applying to college. Just think if he wouldn't have found out about the scholarship requirement until his senior year, after he had already applied. It may have been too late, and he would have missed out on a lot of money.

List some possible businesses you can ask about college scholarship opportunities. Don't forget your local sports teams and legislators.

1)

2)

3)

4)

5)

6)

7)

I currently work at a four-year private school, and a lot of times I get asked if I can offer scholarships based upon FAFSA results. Every school is different. Some schools may take your FAFSA result into consideration. Remember, the FAFSA determines what financial aid you are eligible for based upon what your family is able to contribute toward your education. It mainly determines what you are eligible for based upon need and not merit. Also, the philosophy behind financial aid is that you should pay for your education, and the money that comes from completing the FAFSA is to help you. This means it may not cover the entire cost, so completing a FAFSA without looking into scholarship opportunities is not wise. If you receive scholarships from an outside organization, call each school that you are admitted to and ask how the additional scholarship will affect your financial aid package. This question must be asked, because some scholarships will result in the decrease of your other awards. Every school handles this process differently, so make sure to call so you won't assume your calculations are correct.

This is how the entire process looks:

1. Figure out which schools you are interested in: Reach, Safety, or Guaranteed. (Freshman/Sophomore year is when you should start researching schools)

2. Look into possible scholarships. Make note of requirements and deadlines. (Sophomore/Junior year)

3. Apply to your school choices/scholarships. (Senior year, maybe sooner for some scholarships)

4. Complete FAFSA (Senior year)

5. Await the award package from all of the schools you have been admitted to.

Following this order increases your chances of receiving the most funding for your education. It will also help you to know whether or not you can afford a particular school before you begin. As I have stated throughout this book, it is never too late to try. You are still capable of succeeding. These tips are to help make life easier.

Where are you? Cross out all that have been completed.

Exploration Career/Major/minor	School Options	Campus Visits
College Applications	Scholarships	FAFSA

Do you have any unmarked boxes that need to be completed based upon where you are on your journey or grade level in school? Let's stretch by planning below. Don't forget to work with a parent, advisor, or mentor to make sure you're on the right track.

Goal	To-Do's	Deadline

Some schools will mail you your financial aid award package and others will email you. It is important that you check your mail and email periodically. On the following page is a sample financial aid award package. Let's break it down on the next page.

	Fall (full time)	Spring (full time)	Total
Western Grant	$1,000	$1,000	$2,000
State Grant	$2,360	$2,360	$4,720
Pell Grant	$2,690	$2,690	$5,380
Subsidized Loan	$1,750	$1,750	$3,500
Unsubsidized Loan	$1,000	$1,000	$2,000
Total Aid Awarded	$8,800	$8,800	$17,600

Why Not Stretch University

Estimate Your Out-of-Pocket Expenses

	Fall	Spring	Total
Tuition and Fees (In-State, Full-time)	$5,641	$5,641	$11,283
Room & Board (based on double room rate)	$4,725	$4,725	$9,450
Total estimated out-of-pocket expenses	$1,566	$1,567	$3,133

Parent Loan Eligibility (PLUS)

*After June 1st, your parent may apply online for a PLUS loan.
*Note: Purchase of books requires payment by cash, check, or credit card, and cannot be charged to your university account. You may also have additional expenses throughout the year (student health insurance, telephone charges, lab fees, extra food points).

I wish most financial aid award packages were this user-friendly, however, most are complicated to read. I'm letting you know, so you are aware that it isn't you. Sometimes schools forget that many will be the first to attend college in their families. Even if you are not, things change, so it's important to know that you are not alone and that you should ask as many questions as you would like.

First, the financial aid award package lets the student know the amount of financial aid offered divided between the two semesters. The school I work at, we do not do this. We give the total amount for the year offered. It makes it easy for any family to subtract that amount from one semester's bill. Using myself as an example, when I transferred schools, the school I transferred to showed me my total financial aid for the year. So, naturally, I subtracted a year's worth of financial aid from one semester bill. I was set. Wrong! Since I subtracted the entire package from a semester bill, I thought I had more than enough for school. In actuality, I was supposed to divide the financial aid in half, THEN subtract it from my one semester to come up with what I would owe out of pocket. Whatever I owed for that one semester, I would need to multiply that by two since the aid cuts in half.

This simple mistake of not knowing how your financial aid applies to your bill is a common mistake that leaves many students stuck with a balance that they can't pay after attending school for one semester. Most can't go back due to it.

STRETCH

Some financial aid award packages are estimates (subject to change) and not actual awards. This is typically the case for students who have been selected for a process called verification. Once you've submitted your FAFSA, your school will notify you if you've been selected. For most schools, all that is required to receive financial aid is the FAFSA. However, if you're selected for verification, you have to submit additional documents to the school. The documents that will be requested are to verify that what was reported on the FAFSA is accurate.

After verification is complete, you will be notified whether your financial aid award amount will either remain the same, increase or decrease. This is why it is important to stay on top of all emails sent from the school, and to submit all documentation as soon as possible in order to determine your actual cost to attend said school. You can only properly plan with an actual award and not an estimate.

The Western Grant. This may look different at different schools. The school grant is a gift from the school that is typically based upon your FAFSA results (need-based). Since it is a grant, it may be offered separately from a scholarship (merit-based) that the school may offer.

Not all schools offer what we call institutional aid, but you will not know unless you apply. The amount that a school has to offer its students varies as well, so don't let the price tag discourage you from applying.

Next up is the **Pell Grant**. The Pell Grant may be offered if you are eligible for it. The way your school determines your eligibility for the Pell Grant is by the FAFSA. After you submit your FAFSA, you are given what is called the expected family contribution number (EFC). The EFC is what the school uses to determine what you are eligible for. When it comes to the Federal Pell Grant, your EFC must be below 5000 in order to receive it. Since it is a grant from the federal government, most schools you apply to will offer it to you if you are eligible, unlike state grants.

State Grants are typically only for those students who decide to remain in the state they live in for school. This is why it is important to also apply to in-state schools. The state grants you may receive if you remain in the state you live in may not be an option if you leave the state for school. This doesn't mean other schools may not offer more in institutional funds. It just means that as a safety measure, you should apply to some great in-state schools, just in case.

Next on the financial aid award package is the **subsidized loan**. You may hear people refer to it as a Stafford Loan or Federal Direct Subsidized Loan as well. This loan is a student loan. This means that it is in the student's name. You may receive this loan if your FAFSA results show that you have need. It is a need-based loan where the government pays the interest while you're in school.

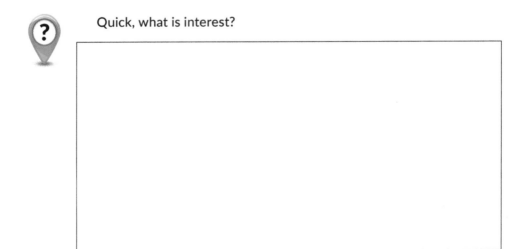

Quick, what is interest?

The loan amount offered is contingent upon what year you are in school. The second student loan that you see is the Federal Direct **Unsubsidized Loan**. This loan is not based upon need. Interest is added while you are in school (so you will pay back more than what you borrowed). You must begin paying both of your loans back six months after you graduate.

Lastly, you may be offered the Parent PLUS Loan. It will be offered as an option (see the above award package where it says "Parent Loan option"). This is very confusing for most students. The way it reads on the package makes it seem as if it is already yours, but it isn't. The Parent PLUS Loan is unlike the student loan because the parent has to pass a credit check to get it. It is a part of the award package to show the student that it is an option, but it isn't guaranteed because there is another step. Since the Department of Education (the federal government, A.K.A the lender) puts a limit on how much a student may borrow from them, they allow the parents to borrow more than what the student needs to attend the school, if they would like, and if their credit is good enough to borrow the loan. Some students' financial aid package is enough to cover their entire bill, but if it isn't, why can't the student borrow enough to cover the entire bill? Well, the government does not allow it. If the parent does not want to borrow a Parent PLUS Loan, and if all of their other aid doesn't cover the entire balance, there is another option that many students choose in order to go to their dream school: the private loan route. Private loans allow the student to borrow more loans to cover the entire cost of their education in their name, if the student's credit check passes. Most students do not have the credit history or work history to get a loan by themselves, so the bank may ask for a cosigner.

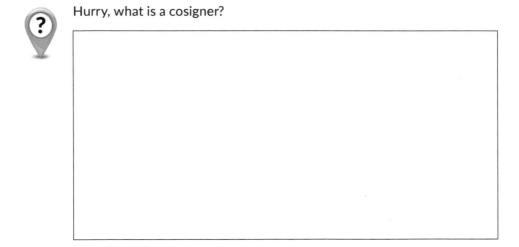

Hurry, what is a cosigner?

I have seen many students begin school with the idea that they will just take out a loan to cover their cost, but it is not that easy. The federal loans you are awarded have limits. If they are not enough to cover your cost, you may apply for a private loan from a bank. The problem with going into school assuming that you will pay the bill with a loan large enough to cover your cost is that it isn't guaranteed to be approved. If you choose the loan route outside of your federal loans, make sure you apply for them and get approved before saying yes to a school, although I strongly recommend you do not attend a school where you will have to borrow private loans.

STRETCH

It is always better to come up with a plan before you say yes to a school. You cannot make plans with money that isn't guaranteed. This includes scholarships. Your plan cannot be to apply for scholarships once you start class. You should be ready to start classes once you know you have been awarded scholarships, and if additional loans will be borrowed, then the process of applying for them (and them being approved) should be done before you say yes to a school. Long story short, do not begin school without knowing how you're going to pay for it. This sounds simple, yet I meet a lot of students who do this, and by the time I meet them, it is too late. They are left with a bill and can't move forward without complete payment.

The private loan industry is why I started this book. They are nothing like the federal subsidized and unsubsidized loans when it comes to repayment or interest rates, but we will dive into this more a little later. Just know that it is an option, just not a smart one in my opinion.

After you receive your financial aid award package, the next step is to come up with what you will have to pay out-of-pocket for each school. First, you should subtract the free money, or what I like to call "gift aid," because you don't have to pay it back. Then, if you are still coming up short, ONLY subtract the subsidized loan if you need to. Loans should be your last resort. The subsidized loan is the better loan of the two federal loans. If you require more assistance, consider the unsubsidized loan.

After you come up with the bottom-line, you should call each school that you were admitted into to make sure your numbers are correct (Learn from my mistake, please). If you still require more financial assistance, my recommendation is to ask the school if they have an APPEALS process to be considered for any additional financial aid options. You would be surprised by how many schools have this option. A closed mouth will not get fed, so open up and ASK!

As a financial aid counselor, I can best assist a totally transparent student. The FAFSA does not give the total story behind your finances. Since this is the case, it is your responsibility to tell me what the circumstance is. Not only should you tell me what your circumstance is, but feel free to discuss your concerns or fears. If your fear is that you will graduate with a lot of debt by using only the federal loans, I could possibly help you to see what repayment will look like for you if you choose to borrow each year in school. Your fear may not be a fear after all, once you are really informed about everything.

Congratulations, you are now an adult in the eyes of the college!

When you enter college, you are considered an adult. Many colleges have excellent resources to help the student do well financially and academically, but it is up to the student to ask about them. Speak up if you have any concerns. Using excuses like not knowing who to ask (ask anyone), or not checking your email will not help you to be successful. The most successful students are those who ask questions and read everything that comes from the school. Knowledge is power, so if you have decided to borrow your federal student loans, make sure you are knowledgeable about them. Remember, when it is time to graduate, you don't want any additional surprises when it comes to repayment. In order to properly plan for when the time comes, make sure you take the time out to ask questions and read up on the federal student loans.

Consider these questions if you've decided to borrow federal student loans:

- Do you know the interest rates for the loans?
- What is your repayment plan after completing school? When are you required to start making payments towards the loans?
- Do you need to borrow the full amount? (Schools may offer the full amount, but it is up to the student to reduce them.)

The biggest mistake is borrowing loans to satisfy a bill, but not taking the time to research the loan. Ask questions. Search the world wide web. Do what you have to so you are not in the dark with your loans.

- Does your school offer payment plans? A payment plan is when you can make monthly payments towards your total cost. This may help prevent you from having to take out a loan.
- Do you have a job? Can you afford to pay the unsubsidized interest while you're in school? This would be wise to do, so that when you graduate, you don't have as much to pay back, but if you cannot, don't stress yourself. Your federal student loans interest is not growing that much in comparison to private loans.

For those who PLAN on working and attending school part-time, you may not need to borrow the full amount of your loans. Make sure you are not over-borrowing since your part-time status means you will be in school longer. Also, make sure you are attending a school that doesn't require you to use as many loans to attend part-time as you would if you attended full-time. In order for you to make sure your financial aid lasts, talk about what you should and shouldn't borrow for all of your school expenses with a financial aid advisor because, again, financial aid does not last forever.

STRETCH

After you accept the federal loans, you must complete Entrance Counseling. A lot of students run through this requirement to get it over with, but it is there to help you better understand the responsibility of borrowing the loan. Take your time and work through the counseling so you are well informed of the decision you are making.

If you need to explore private loan options in order to attend your dream school, I would recommend that you choose another school. Private loans typically do not have the many different repayment options that federal loans have. You must think about life after college. You will want your own place, car, ability to travel, etc. Federal loans are typically more manageable, and their interest rates are fixed. Fixed loans are loans with interest rates that will not increase. Private loans, on the other hand, are not subject to the same rules. Most private loans have interest rates that can go up at any point, making it very hard to plan what your repayment will look like. Typically, private loans do not offer a variety of repayment plans. This means if you are unemployed, making minimum wage, or decide to go back to school, you will still be required to pay hundreds of dollars a month towards your loan payment.

I was working full-time when I decided to attend a four-year school, so I was able to apply for private loans. If I knew then what I know now, I would have gone to another school. My private loans did not care that my income was at an impoverished level when I graduated. They still demanded $400.00 a month. If I didn't pay that and only paid what I could, they would send me to collections, which means my credit would begin to decline. I would not be able to apply for a home, car, or even a credit card at that (not that I needed it, but you get it).

A few sample award packages can be found on the following pages. Complete the calculations for both schools with and without the loans.

College A:

Costs for the 2017-18 Academic Year	
Estimated costs of attendance for full-time enrollment	$41,972/year
Tuition and Fees	$26,470
Room and Board (average)	$9,494
Books and Supplies	$1,300
Transportation	$2,680
Other educational expenses	$2,028
Your grants and scholarships to pay for college	
Total grants and scholarships to pay for college	$6,670
Grants and scholarships from your school	$3,000
Federal Pell Grant	$3,670
Grants from your state	$0
Other scholarships	$0
What will you pay for college?	
Net costs (Cost of attendance minus total grants and scholarships)	
Options to pay for net costs	
Loan options	
Federal Direct Subsidized Loan	$3,500
Federal Direct Unsubsidized Loan	$2,000
Federal Parent Plus Loan	$29,802
Net cost (Cost of attendance minus total grants, scholarships, and loans)	

College B:

Costs for the 2017-18 Academic Year	
Estimated costs of attendance for full-time enrollment	$56,800
Tuition and Fees	$38,900
Room and Board (average)	$13,800
Books and Supplies	$1,300
Transportation	$1,400
Other educational expenses	$1,400
Your grants and scholarships to pay for college	
Total grants and scholarships to pay for college	$35,000
Grants and scholarships from your school	$26,610
Federal Pell Grant	$3,670
Grants from your state	$4,720
Other scholarships	$0
What will you pay for college?	
Net costs (Cost of attendance minus total grants and scholarships)	
Options to pay for net costs	
Loan options	
Federal Direct Subsidized Loan	$3,500
Federal Direct Unsubsidized Loan	$2,000
Federal Parent Plus Loan	$29,802
Net cost (Cost of attendance minus total grants, scholarships, loans)	

? Which school would you attend and why?

[blank response box]

Now that you have calculated your bottom line at both schools, let's discuss, compare, and contrast. Without doing any calculations, I can tell that College A is an out-of-state school. There is nothing wrong with applying out-of-state, but like I stated previously, you will definitely want to apply to some in-state schools, since the state grant you see on College B's award package is not on College A's. Also, naturally, it is safe to assume that College A is cheaper just by looking at the sticker price, however, College B may look more expensive, but who gave the most money? College B. You would not have known this unless you applied to both schools!

Before we get into what it will cost you, the first thing I would ask the school is which of the fees listed are mandatory and which are a part of your direct cost – what is the bill? The books and supplies, transportation and other may be expenses you will need to consider (especially books), but what will you owe the school? My calculations will only include the tuition and fees and room and board. Here is what I got for your expected cost from both schools:

	College A	College B
Without Loans	$29,294	$17,700
With Subsidized Loan *$3,500-1.069%= $3,462	$25,832	$14,238
With both Sub and Unsub Loans *$5,500-1.069%=$5,441	$23,853	$12,259

Whenever you borrow federal student loans, the Department of Education charges an origination fee. This is what it costs to process the loan. You don't have to make a payment to them to cover it; they will take it off the top of your loans. This means that if the origination fee is 1.069%, then that's how much they will remove from your loan. If you borrow the full amount of $5,500 then what will actually go to the school is $5,441.

Now that we have come up with how much you will owe as a full-time student, if you plan on going part-time, you will need to call the financial aid office to discuss how your aid will change, because it will reduce. Keep in mind, going part-time so you can afford your dream school is not a wise decision (part-time = being in school longer = more expensive). Your next step is to contact the school and ask to see if there are any additional ways of obtaining more funding. If they have an appeals process, complete it as soon as possible and turn it in.

Once you hear back from the school about any additional funding, recalculate your bottom line. If the price is still too much, you may want to play around with the option of not staying on campus and commuting to class from home. If this is an option for you, you will need to contact the financial aid office to see if your financial aid will change if you do not stay on campus. Some schools will reduce your aid, others will not. For those that will not, if you removed housing from your bill for College B, you would end up owing $3,900 for the year without loans. Without housing, you could pay the difference out-of-pocket or only borrow the subsidized loan. You're paying $3,900 for your education at a school that charges $38,900. Now do you see why it pays to not look at the sticker price?

Work Study. What about work study? Well, I didn't mention it prior to now because it confuses a lot of families. When Work Study is listed on the financial aid award package, some families make the mistake of taking the amount and subtracting it from the direct cost. This gives the family an incorrect number for what they will have to pay out-of-pocket. Federal Work-Study is a program that is given to students who are eligible based upon the student's FAFSA. In order for you to use it, you must apply for an on-campus job. Once you get the on-campus job, they will use the federal work study money to pay you. If you do not obtain an on-campus job, then nothing happens to it. Long story short, the many offices on campus may require that you are work-study eligible before hiring you because they do not have funds to pay you themselves, so they use the federal government's funds that they have for such jobs to pay student workers.

I want to make sure you know what to do after you receive your financial aid award package. It's important that you determine the bottom line. This is a CRUCIAL step, a step that many overlook. You receive your acceptance letter and are excited that you have been accepted into your dream school, and you tell the school you are going to attend without considering the cost. This happens a lot, trust me. I'm here to make sure you attend a good school that will not leave you broke. I have seen too many dream schools turn into nightmares because the student said yes, then asked questions last. If you do some proper planning, apply for scholarships, and start your college admission process in a timely manner, you are more likely to be prepared academically and financially for the school of your choice. Apply to them all and then make sure you make the best decision for you.

Now that you have a basic understanding of how financial aid works, let's go over some frequent myths I hear regarding financial aid.

1. Financial aid will cover the entire cost.

   A. True
   B. False
   C. Both

   The answer is (C) both. Depending on the school and your efforts to apply for scholarships, you may have enough to cover the entire cost. This is not always the case, so it is important that after you get your financial aid package, you determine the cost you will need to pay out-of-pocket. Keep in mind that the purpose of financial aid is to assist families with the cost. This does not mean it will cover everything.

2. I can borrow loans in my name to cover the entire cost.

   A. True
   B. False
   C. Both

   The answer is (C) both. The federal loans that will be a part of your financial aid award package could be just what you need to attend the school of choice. In some cases, it is not, because the government does place limits on what you can borrow from them. The private loan you may consider if approved, that I disagree with, can cover the total cost.

STRETCH

If your outstanding yearly balance without loans is $5000 and your student loans equal $5500, then your loans are more than what you need to attend the school. If your balance is $10,000 for the year without loans and your loans total $5500, then your loans reduce your out-of-pocket cost, but don't cover the entire balance.

3. The price on the school's website is the amount I will have to pay.

A. True
B. False

The answer is (B) false. If you complete the FAFSA, you will receive some financial aid that will help to reduce the cost. You will not know what that is until after you get your financial aid award package, so apply anyway.

4. You will receive the same amount of financial aid at each school you apply to.

A. True
B. False

The answer is (B) false. Remember, the institutional aid you may receive is what that school can give you. This will not be the same at each school. Your federal aid should be the same at every school as well as your state aid (if you remain in your state). If you did not receive the same federal or state aid at a for-profit school that you did at a nonprofit, then you know that the for-profit school (no matter how enticing they may be) is not a good option.

5. Is it wise to ask questions?

    A. True
    B. False

(A) True! Financial aid can be confusing. It is not you! Ask questions like these:
*   What is included in the cost as a full-time or part-time student? Tuition, fees, room, board, books?
*   How much will I owe each quarter/semester out-of-pocket if I didn't borrow loans?
*   How much will I owe each semester if I borrowed the subsidized loan only?
*   How much will I owe each semester if I borrowed both loans?
*   Can I reduce my loans? Do I need the full amount?
*   Do you have an appeals process?
*   Is the aid that I was offered guaranteed each year I'm in school?
*   What is required to renew my financial aid each year (specifically institutional aid in the form of grants and scholarships, if applicable)?

- How much does tuition increase each year?
- Are there additional scholarship opportunities available?
- Can I schedule an appointment to meet with you?

Sometimes it is best to visit the office to ask your questions. Financial aid offices can be hectic around certain times of the year. In the event you can't make it on campus, you should not hesitate to sit with your mentor or high school counselor and make a phone call to the school so you can have someone assist you with asking questions.

After I transferred from my community college to the school I graduated from, I made a lot of mistakes. I misread the website and thought that the amount listed was for the full year, but it wasn't. I didn't ask questions initially and by the time I did, I had a huge balance. I wish I would have asked a mentor to assist me with getting answers because I was more confused when I left the office. After I realized I couldn't pay, I stopped attending class because I made it up in my mind that I would just go to the army, even though that's not what I really wanted.

Once I decided not to go that route, I then worked to pay off my balance. I worked three jobs and sold my car to get back into school, all because I didn't ask questions before I agreed to transfer, and I didn't properly plan, as I assumed that I knew what I was doing. Don't be like me. You can never ask enough questions. You see, you may not know everything about financial aid or the college-going process, but if you know enough to stay on top of the essentials, then you are on the right track to making the best decision for your life. The essentials are your goals and the bill. The bill must be paid, so how are you going to pay? Do you have enough to cover your direct cost? Will you have to pay for books and supplies?

Why not Stretch

 Oftentimes, you will find that the difference between the college graduate and the college drop-out is one's ability to stretch beyond barriers. Everything that I faced while in college due to how I aimlessly went about my high school career should have made me a drop-out too. However, once I made it up in my mind that life with a college degree was better than a life without one, my answer to the question: "Why not stretch?" was, "Why not?" I know it isn't grammatically correct to answer a question with a question, but the answer made me think about what it was I had to lose by stretching – nothing.

I understand that there are some students who may have to stretch a little more than the next. Completing a FAFSA may be a simple step to some but complicated for the next, depending on your familial background. A parent loan may or may not be an option for you either. It is my hope that whatever the circumstance, you take your community and begin to plan routes around those barriers. You do not allow those barriers to prevent you from attacking your goal. So, as simple as I made some of the steps seem, I acknowledge that it isn't simple for everyone, but with the right amount of confidence to ask questions, be transparent, build a community, explore, and properly plan, I believe you can stretch beyond them.

When I began writing this workbook, I was angry. Now, as I visualize a student reading this workbook and taking the necessary steps to not only dream big but stretch big, I can only smile. So, I'm no longer angry. I've stretched beyond others' expectations of me, and I continue to stretch beyond the mistakes I've made. You can, too! Although I didn't become a dentist – I found out later on that my disdain for germs would prevent me from enjoying that profession – I have been able to complete my master's degree by having it paid for in full, and now my doctorate degree is being paid for. I still have my student loan debt, but I'm happy knowing that my mistakes may possibly prevent someone else from borrowing large, life-altering debt.

The confidence I've gained from speaking up has helped me to learn more about budgeting my money and payments so that I may now have a life. Throughout this workbook, I'm only telling you what I am challenging myself to continue to do. I'm making the best out of my circumstance. I'm stretching. I've created value in my faults, and I'm happier now more than ever. So, here is an early congratulations to you for taking charge of your life. May you consistently enjoy the journey of stretching beyond your circumstance.

Acknowledgements

To my parents, Claude and Kerri Massey, thank you, thank you, thank you! Thank you for the support, encouragement, and love throughout every mistake I've made. You two never made me feel like I was a disappointment. Just knowing that I wasn't a failure in your eyes, despite how the real world tried to make me feel, helped me to put one foot in front of the other, every single time. I never gave up because I have never seen you two give up. I was born with the Massey tenacity, and I'm forever grateful.

To my siblings, Tarita and Edward Massey, who gave me whatever money they could to make sure my needs were met, I thank you. Just know that me asking you for money will probably never end no matter what.

Last, but certainly not least, to my husband, Emanuel A. Smith Jr. Thank you for continuously praying for and with me. Your prayers helped to push me to turn my mistakes into purpose, and I'm indebted to you for that.

Stretching Toward College Acceptance

You can do it!

Explore!

Make new friends!

Get a Mentor!

Freshman Year

Goal	Due Date	Completed
Explore careers		☐
Join clubs		☐
Build your communities		☐

Sophomore Year

Goal	Due Date	Completed
Research career requirements *major, minor, time commitment, etc.		☐
Research colleges *Admission & scholarship requirements & deadlines		☐

Junior Year

Goal	Due Date	Completed
Meet with college mentor/counselor	October	☐
College tour(s)		☐
Narrow down your list of college choices *Take note of admission and scholarship deadlines* *Application cost or application fee waiver process* *Application requirements*	January	☐
Search for external scholarships	February	☐
Take standardized test	March	☐

Research

Stretch

Senior Year

Goal	Due Date	Completed
Retake standardized test *If applicable*	August	☐

Senior Year (Cont.)

Goal	Due Date	Completed
Submit college application(s)		☐
Complete FAFSA	October 1st	☐
Apply for additional scholarships	November	☐

CONGRATULATIONS!
You've been admitted.

Goal	Due Date	Completed
Receive financial aid award(s)		☐
Determine bottom line		☐
Make your decision *submit your deposit	May 1st	☐

Check email

Ask questions

Stretch

CPSIA information can be obtained
at www.ICGtesting.com
Printed in the USA
LVHW070347210521
688045LV00015B/994

9 781645 382256